T0381039

Flameless Liquid CREMATION

HAL PETERS

Archway Publishing books may be ordered through booksellers or by contacting:

Archway Publishing
1663 Liberty Drive
Bloomington, IN 47403
www.archwaypublishing.com
844-669-3957

Because of the dynamic nature of the Internet, any web addresses or links contained in this book may have changed since publication and may no longer be valid. The views expressed in this work are solely those of the author and do not necessarily reflect the views of the publisher, and the publisher hereby disclaims any respon-sibility for them.

ISBN: 978-1-6657-3184-3 (sc)
ISBN: 978-1-6657-3185-0 (hc)
ISBN: 978-1-6657-3186-7 (e)

Library of Congress Control Number: 2022919170

Print information available on the last page.

Archway Publishing rev. date: 12/02/2022

TABLE OF CONTENTS

DEDICATION

In recognition of the legacy left to us by Desmond Tutu.

Even in this area, you have shown us the way.

FOREWORD

When we brought the idea of alkaline hydrolysis to the funeral industry in 1998, there was virtually no interest in it. It had been used in the Willed Body program at Shands Hospital at the University of Florida since 1995. In 2005, Mayo Clinic decided to replace their crumbling incinerator with a single body human system that we designed and built in our company, WR2. This created some visibility for the idea of a single body alkaline hydrolysis system that could be used for human use.

Years later, on January 26, 2011, the first human body from a funeral home in Ohio was used and history was made. Since that time, alkaline hydrolysis has been approved in five Canadian provinces, twenty-six states in the United States, South Africa, and Mexico. More than 400 human and pet systems are operating around the world every day.

As people learn about the process, more and more funeral homes, cemeteries, and crematories are starting to use the technology.

When given the choice, over 80 percent of people prefer the idea of Flameless Liquid Cremation (also referred to as FLC) to flame-based cremation. Flameless Liquid Cremation has only a ten percent environmental impact, as compared to flame-based cremation, which uses fossil fuels.

As the late R. Brian Burkhardt, author of *Rest in Peace: Insider's Tips to the Low Cost Less Stress Funeral*, said after seeing the process performed in 2011, "You have no idea the impact you will have on the funeral industry."

Late last year, Archbishop Desmond Tutu chose to go through our Aquamation™ alkaline hydrolysis system in Cape Town, South Africa, citing his feeling that it is the most environmentally benign way to pass into the next life. Well Mr. Burkhardt, you were right: we really did not know the impact this would have. Ten years later, we have a good idea that it *will* continue to grow in popularity.

I hope you enjoy this book as much as I did.

- Joe Wilson, CEO, Bio-Response Solutions, Inc.

PREFACE

We do not have the liberty to choose the time we come into this world or when we leave, but we *do* have authority over deciding about our "melting away" from this world.

The methods of disposing of a human body have evolved, and today *we have more options*. Although the age-old in-ground burial and cremation practices are still widely followed, there is a newer, more palatable/agreeable way to handle the human remains disposal process.

Nowadays, people are much more aware of their surroundings and their impact on the environment. The "carbon footprint," a term that was once used only by environmentalists, is becoming an essential topic of discussion in large organizations, schools, and even homes.

All this has led people to choose a *new* process called Flameless Liquid Cremation over other ways to "go." It is sometimes also called Aquamation or Alkaline Hydrolysis. This option offers a process for human body disposal that is an improvement on many levels.

- It is a better choice for the environment.

- It is more economical.

- It offers a person more serenity and tranquility when anticipating the long-term future.

- It offers flexibility, e.g., "burial" at sea for everyone.

As Ernest Hemmingway once supposedly observed, "Every man's life ends the same way. It is only the details of how he lived and how he died that distinguish one man from another."

Enabled by this new technology, our one last decision may serve to create a strong impact on how we leave this world.

Even though the responsibility of disposing of the bodies of their loved ones lies with relatives and friends, it is difficult to make this decision on behalf of the person they loved so much. It is better to make *your* wishes known. In this way, they have guidance on what *you* want done with *your* body.

In fact, experts advise also taking matters into your hands in other realms, such as:

- Your financial affairs by writing a will; and

- Your medical wishes by drafting a directive to specify in what manner, and to what extent, you want extraordinary machine-assisted procedures to be used, and for how long.

Recently, Desmond Tutu, Nobel Peace Prize winner (1984) and human rights activist in South Africa, chose Flameless Liquid Cremation as his choice of body disposal after his death. This is detailed in Chapter 4.

Flameless Liquid Cremation is an environmentally friendly, economical, and 100 percent sanitary option for human body disposal.

In this book, I will discuss what Flameless Liquid Cremation is, how the complete process works, and how it helps the environment as a person's last carbon footprint.

This book also aims to help you understand what the human body goes through after our consciousness has left our physical limits. By no means is this book about peoples' spiritual journeys. Rather, we will venture into the more scientific side of human life and death.

By the end of this book, you will be more knowledgeable about this new end-of-life option. The intent is to introduce you to more palatable, uplifting, and ultimately more positive ways of thinking about, and dealing with, the human body after death.

CHAPTER 1

Introduction to Flameless Liquid Cremation

Flameless Liquid Cremation is not a new process for disposal. Cattle and horses have been cremated using this method for a long time now. In fact, this method is currently also used across the United States for the disposal of pets.

Let us investigate the history of how this process originated.

Flameless Liquid Cremation was invented by a farmer named Amos Herbert Hobson in the 1880s. At that time, it was used to make fertilizer from animal carcasses. When an outbreak of Bovine spongiform encephalopathy (more commonly known as mad cow disease) occurred in the 1990s, people found that using the Flameless Liquid Cremation process was the only effective and safe way of handling the herds that needed to be euthanized.

In 1993, Albany Medical College was the first to install a commercial Aquamation system. In order to understand Liquid Flameless Cremation, it is vital to recognize the differences between this process and that of using a flame / fire.

Environmental Impact of Regular Cremation versus Flameless Liquid Cremation

The regular flame-based cremation process vaporizes water content and soft tissue and turns the bones (skeleton) into ashes. The body is burned in a closed furnace (called a retort) for about two to three hours. It requires the temperature to be 1,400°F to 1,800°F (760°C to 980°C). This consumes a lot of energy. Besides being energy intensive, the process has the potential of emitting toxic chemicals into the air (e.g., mercury from dental fillings).

Flameless Liquid Cremation uses water and alkaline chemicals to naturally break down the human body, which essentially liquefies everything except the bones. This process takes several hours, depending on the equipment's temperature and the weight of the body. Some people look upon cremation as an analogous decomposition process to what the human body goes through after a burial, except that cremation speeds up the process.

The Flameless Cremation Process is considered eco-friendly for the following reasons.

1. It does not release any carbon emissions.
2. It does not pollute the air.
3. Medical implants can be recycled because they do not melt during the Liquid Cremation process.
4. Liquid Cremation has a carbon footprint that is one-tenth that of flame cremation.
5. It does not need wood or natural gas for the cremation process.
6. No embalming fluid will leak into the groundwater.
7. No cement structures need to be manufactured and buried in the ground around a casket. In fact, there is no casket, no headstone, and no need to keep the grave ground maintained, and so on.

One can look upon selecting Flameless Liquid Cremation as one last contribution to the environment, a gesture toward a greener planet and reduced pollution. The process uses 95 percent water and 5 percent alkali to dissolve the soft tissue of the body. As with flame-based cremation, the bones remain after the process has been completed and must be dried, converted into powdered form, placed in an urn (usually a little larger than the one used in flame-based cremation), and then disposed of appropriately.

The alkali used for Flameless Liquid Cremation is classified as a base chemical. It is *not* acid (which has a pH between 1 and 6). Alkali is commonly used in antacid stomach remedies, and it is often used in cosmetics, body washes, soap, shampoo, and shaving creams.

Although the alkaline chemicals used during Flameless Liquid Cremation are not acidic, they are very caustic. They have to be in order to do the job of melting a person's soft tissue into its basic components.

Striving to help the environment is just one of the reasons people elect FLC.

Practitioners have noted that people also choose FLC because it is viewed as a comparatively more gentle process. Many feel more assured that they can now bid farewell to the world in a nicer way. Additionally, Flameless Liquid Cremation is sometimes preferred because of the fear of fire. Even though the human body does not feel pain after death, fire is still a cause of anxiety for some people as they play out the various scenarios in their minds.

Making the decision to have FLC done might help someone come to terms with death. The author himself states as much.

Legalization of Flameless Liquid Cremation

The legalization of FLC for human use in the United States has been spotty. So far, only twenty-six states have fully legalized this process (see Appendix B). As can be anticipated, there was a lot of resistance and political battles from vested interests in each state before FLC was adopted.

Since funeral and cemetery laws are not in the hands of the federal government, each state must decide whether it would like to authorize this option for human body disposal.

Since FLC makes no noise, does not spew smoke and fumes, and consumes minimal energy, this equipment can be placed practically anywhere. In fact, there are funeral parlors in residential areas that are successfully deploying/converting to this business model.

As we speak, several states are in the process of legalizing Flameless Liquid Cremation, which will pave the way to building more of these types of cremation centers. This will, in turn, provide more access for the public (that will be increasingly asking for it).

Shipping bodies out of state is now the only way to have this process done for many who desire it.

In the United States, over 50 percent of people who die are now being cremated, using mostly the existing flame-based approach.

As FLC will become more widely known, the economic drivers for selecting cremation will continue, but the method of cremation will, some predict, mostly *switch over* to FLC.

With this rising trend toward cremation in general, it is evident that Americans are not stuck with in-ground or above-ground internment approaches. Many are open to other options for disposal of family members and may ultimately select FLC for themselves as well.

CHAPTER 2

Flameless Liquid Cremation—The Details

We have established that FLC is a "green" process and how it is eco-friendly. Let's now look at the process in more detail.

Of course, it is a delicate and complex topic to discuss. The passing away of our loved ones is never easy, and having this discussion with your relatives can be overwhelming, not to mention depressing.

However, this is a meaningful discussion that should not be left for the last moments of life.

When people research options for their burial, most people—once they find out about FLC and if it is available in their locale—will, we predict, settle upon Flameless Liquid Cremation. This is because it seems more soothing, gentler, and more comforting than other options.

People in the process of making this decision for themselves or a family member should, of course, do their homework. They should investigate and understand the workings of Flameless Liquid Cremation and how and why it might be a preferred option. This is especially true if a person has spent his or her life being cautious about his or her carbon footprint. In such cases, one certainly should not stop caring about the environment when it is time to make this last decision.

Be aware that what we call Flameless Liquid Cremation is known by several other names, such as alkaline hydrolysis, green cremation, and water cremation. Some marketing terms used for this process are Aquamation™, Biocremation™ and Resomation™.

Legal terms sometimes used for Flameless Liquid Cremation are chemical disposition and dissolution.

No matter which of these terms is used, they all involve basically the same process. Additionally, the scientific term hydrolysis refers to the process of a body breaking down because of water (mixed with hydroxide).

Now for the process itself, which might vary slightly from state to state.

Flameless Liquid Cremation requires four things: water, a small fan to move the water and make it flow, some heat (which induces some pressure), and a hydrolysis alkaline chemical. It is crucial to know that even though it is a cremation process, the *decomposition* of the body replicates and parallels what happens via burial. Decomposition via the burial method, however, moves at a much slower pace, for what occurs underground happens over many years.

The Flameless Liquid Cremation process begins with the body being transported to the facility. It is safely stored, identified, and tracked. The process requires special equipment and training from a regulated body. There is no need for embalming the body; there is no need for a casket; there is no need for clothing (a shroud or silken sheet is all that is required).

A single chamber machine, which is airtight and watertight, is used for the process.

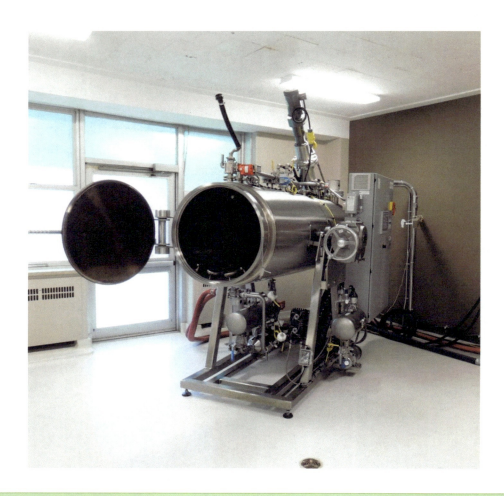

Typical equipment that does Flameless Liquid Cremation for humans. (Since there are no fumes, no need for a Natural Gas supply, no noise, etc. . . . These machines have even been set-up in Funeral Homes that are in residential areas.)

New technological wonder in end-of-life approaches. In the future, most Americans won't be buried... they will dissolve.

Pets (and their owners) will not spend decades in a grave in the ground, but in a few hours soaked in softly circulating Alkalinized water.

History of Flameless Water Cremation, Aquamation, Alkaline Hydrolysis

About 50% of US States have already fully approved the process for humans

This process is currently being used for pets

Animal husbandry has been using it for a long time to dispose of dead cattle, dead horses, etc. (since 1888).

The chamber contains liquid (about 150 gallons). The chamber is sealed after the body is placed inside. A solution of water and alkaline chemicals is entered into the sealed chamber. The amount of the solution required depends on the body mass and weight of the deceased. Once the chamber is filled up with water and the alkaline chemical, a propeller is used to gently stir the water around inside the unit. Complete decomposition can take from four to sixteen hours. The time it takes depends on two factors:

1. The equipment type used (i.e., how much heat the machine uses); and
2. The person's weight and body mass.

The solution prepared for the process is a combination of 95 percent water and 5 percent alkaline chemicals. The chemicals used in the process are potassium hydroxide, sodium hydroxide, or a combination of the two.

After completing the process, only a light tea-colored effluent liquid and bone fragments are left of the person who once lived and breathed. The effluent liquid left behind is sterile and contains sugar, salt, minerals, amino acids, and peptides. The liquid is diluted with over a hundred additional gallons of rinse water and a co-flush (to cool it). Because it is 100 percent sterile, most practitioners simply, and legally, dispose of it into the city drainage system (for it causes no harm).

The author proposes that if practitioners are near one of the coasts, they think about the benefits of incorporating into their best practices or standard operating procedures the *disposition of **all*** effluent directly into the ocean.

If a cremation facility is *not* near one of the coasts, those practitioners will have no choice but to pour the effluent down the drain. All involved must realize that the drain winds up in a treatment plant, and that water then eventually does go out to some type of flowing stream or river. The atoms of the deceased *ultimately* do wind up in an ocean, but in a roundabout manner.

The bone fragments left behind are dried and then crushed to ashes. The family can choose to have the ashes returned to them. They can choose to scatter the ashes, keep the urn at home, put the urn into a bank safe deposit box, or some other option. There have been dozens of ways people have found to creatively manage what happens to the contents of the urn. If the family so desires, the urn's contents can be also emptied and cast onto the water, at the same time the effluent liquid is processed.

Once a body goes through the process of Flameless Liquid Cremation, there are no traces left of DNA.

It should be reiterated that Flameless Liquid Cremation is a very hygienic, sterile, and a safe to handle process. The entire body decomposes, including all the components of the DNA. In fact, the European Union deemed it the *only* safe way to dispose of cow carcasses back when mad cow disease was prevalent. The reason was that this is the *only* process that results in 100 percent safe and sanitary disposal.

In summary, the FLC option is a more gentle way to bid farewell. Those Americans who have heard of it have preferred and selected it in increasing numbers. It is considered a loving and caring way to put your loved ones to rest. Bluntly speaking, it is an efficient and effective way to dispose of the deceased.

CHAPTER 3

Burial at Sea

Let's discuss what burial at sea means within the context of Flameless Liquid Cremation.

Many people are fond of the concept of sea burials. The process appears peaceful, calming, and comforting for both the deceased and the loved ones seeing them off. Additionally, the mystique around the ocean and the serene beauty of the place makes it an excellent choice as a final resting place for any human being—as opposed to a crowded cemetery (see page 12).

Because it is important, we want to again stress that for those Flameless Liquid Cremation practitioners who are located near one of the coasts, we highly recommend that they incorporate, as part of their regular business practices, the transporting of *all* the effluent to a boat, which will take it out to sea. This will facilitate the FLC practice becoming *the* dominant approach!

For those facilities that are in the middle of the country, those practitioners will have no choice but to pour the effluent down the drain. All must realize, however, that the drain winds up in a treatment plant, and that water then eventually goes out to some type of flowing stream or river. Yes, the atoms of these deceased people also *ultimately* wind up in an ocean.

In effect, burial at sea will be the standard procedure for all

For those near one of the coasts

Being cast into the water is a beautiful visual, one that puts your mind to rest when you think about the last time your body components were, more or less, closely together. Would it not be splendid to bid this world farewell by entering a serene environment, such as winding up in the ocean?

Often, for logistical reasons, loved ones cannot be by your side during this process to witness this last journey.

In such cases, the relatives of the deceased's family should be given the option to witness the last moments of their loved ones virtually. There should be regular (and fully included in the price of the services offered) procedures put in place, to videotape the process.

The key steps can be videotaped with empathy and care. This video should not be accessible by people other than the family. It should be uploaded onto a secure server, where only the family can access it or download it. They should be able to access and view it at any time.

If the family elects to keep the video, they might even choose to share this archival record at a service with friends and relatives in attendance. Emotionally, there are benefits for families to *not* opt out of having an observance after the cremation. The grieving process is hard enough, without an ability to have formal closure.

Planning should go into whether the final goodbye service is a home visitation, at a funeral parlor, or an outside memorial event.

The website DignityMemorial.com states

> Whether small or large, formal or casual, a memorial or celebration of life brings people together to remember their loved one, connect over the good times, comfort one another, and begin the healing process.
>
> End-of-life ceremonies are an important part of being human, and the comfort of joining with others in grief—sharing tears and laughter—can be a vital part of the healing process.[1]

Effluent Liquid Usage Options

Since the liquid effluent is safe to handle and contains many nutrients, some families might want to ask for one gallon of it, to be used by them around the back yard.

The liquid could be poured around trees and bushes, in order to fully feel close to the loved one. If sprinkled evenly, it will not negatively affect plant life, grass, or other plant and animal life.

In this way, the essence of the person will take on life in the items growing in the back yard.

---

[1] Dignity Memorial, "How Long Does a Cremation Take?", Dignity Memorial, accessed September 28, 2022, https://www.dignitymemorial.com/plan-funeral-cremation/cremation/timeline.

Looks jam-packed . . . doesn't it?

The Snow Covered Sign Says . . . "Dead End".
The image conjures up lying in a cold grave, once the road ends.

**Burial at sea! It is like "Going Home" . . .
(to where long ago, our evolutionary
ancestors came from)**

Flameless Liquid Cremation . . . is not "Dust to dust" . . . but "Dust to water" for EVERYONE!

Burial at sea –or- burial into a stream / river (that will EVENTUALLY bring the effluent liquid to an Ocean)!

Handling of the Urn's Contents

Similar to regular/traditional cremation, Flameless Liquid Cremation also uses an urn. This urn contains the pulverized bones of the deceased. Comparatively, this urn is bigger than a standard urn from the traditional flame-based process because there are more ashes. These ashes, much like the leftover effluent liquid, are also 100 percent safe and sterile.

In case the family cannot come to pick up the urn, they have the option to have it shipped via a registered delivery service. From there, it is up to the family to either scatter the remains of their loved one in a cemetery, a favorite vacation spot, under a tree to be planted in their back yard, or another location. They can even choose to keep the urn in their home as memorabilia if they wish. They may choose to have it interred (i.e., safely placed) into a bank deposit box or placed within a special cemetery unit called a columbarium. This is a dedicated structure with niches for placement of cremated remains housed in urns. A columbarium may be outdoors, in its own building, or in a separate wing of a mausoleum. A wall columbarium usually holds many urns behind glass doors.

There are many creative options for honoring the life of the individual.

The family may wish to have the ashes disposed of at the same time as the liquid effluent is poured into the sea. In that case, they can notify the management of the crematorium, and they will make sure to scatter the ashes into the ocean along with the liquid.

As more people have been choosing cremation (regular flame-based and, in the future, Flameless Liquid), more options for the urn's contents have become available. There are now many choices that offer soothing and comfort. There are various things one can choose to do with ashes. Some include:

- Putting the ashes into fireworks;

- Scattering them over the graves of one's parents;

- Having some of it made into jewelry;

- Having a portrait or other artwork made using some of the cremation remains; and

- Burying the ashes in a biodegradable container and planting a tree in the location.

In addition to all this, in the coming years the world will move forward with giant leaps, and humankind will be able to choose the moon as a final destination. Currently, contractors with NASA are working on this project, and eventually people will be able to land on the moon and stay there after they have passed away from this world.

A best practice process for a burial at sea might look something like this.

1. The boat drops anchor at a spot that is three or more nautical miles away from the shore.
2. Video recording begins. The date, time, and GPS location are shown on a cell phone for the camera. Since these are important moments that the family would want to have captured, documenting the process in as precise a manner as possible is important. Hence, understanding these sentiments, the people handling the sea burial must ensure that every detail is recorded clearly.
3. Once the recording begins, a wreath is thrown into the sea in respect and honor of the deceased. It must be noted that the wreath used must be degradable, so it doesn't harm the marine life.
4. The effluent liquid is then poured into the water. The liquid is contained in plastic barrels brought from the crematorium directly. If the family has specified that the ashes should be scattered into the sea as well, then after the effluent is poured, the staff handling the process will scatter all the ashes into the ocean, and the process comes to an end.

The whole process is respectful and beautiful.

The crematorium will show respect and honor for the deceased by ensuring that every step is lovingly recorded. The family can view it and be at peace knowing that their loved one is now in a place of serenity. The deceased has fully completed his or her journey in this world successfully.

Watching a loved one leave the world in this way can surely bring some closure and peace to the family members' hearts, especially in knowing that the person has chosen this for himself or herself and that his or her request has been respected and fulfilled.

CHAPTER 4

Desmond Tutu

By now, hopefully you better understand what Flameless Liquid Cremation is, and why people might prefer it over other ways of disposition. You might even be considering this for yourself. After all, how we choose to leave this world should be our own choice. This burden should not have to fall upon family members, who must cope with the loss of a loved one, arrange for a service, and speak to people about how to best honor the person they just lost.

We do not want to add extra stress to an already overwhelming experience. We can clarify this important aspect of life by thinking through how we wish to depart from this world and communicate our wishes prior to our deaths.

Desmond Tutu, the South African environmentalist and statesman, decided what would happen to his body and communicated it before his death took place. He elected Flameless Liquid Cremation.

You may be familiar with his name and work. If not, then let us tell you about this great man. He spearheaded a truth and reconciliation process and was instrumental in saving South Africa from descending into chaos after the end of Apartheid.

Inadvertently, his celebrity is also having ongoing influence by shedding light on the process of Flameless Liquid Cremation. He continues to have a large impact on the world, by bringing this approach to light, even outside of South Africa.

He wore many hats. Desmond Tutu was a South African archbishop and an effective and influential human rights activist. He was appointed as Dean of St. Mary's Cathedral in Johannesburg in 1975 and was the first black person to receive this honor.

Tutu believed in building a democratic world with equal rights and freedom from racial discrimination. He won the Nobel Peace Prize in 1984 for being a unifier and a respected leader, and by eloquently advocating for positive, non-violent campaigns and protests.

Despite such outstanding achievements, Tutu was a very humble man. One of his passions was his concern for the environment. It is no surprise that this intelligent man chose to leave this world through the practice of Flameless Liquid Cremation.

Desmond Tutu was a global figure and, as per tradition, received a grand and momentous funeral. He acted, before his death, to communicate an important decision. He let it be known that he wanted the Flameless Liquid Cremation process performed when the time came.

Suppose he had not shared his wish. People would still have given him an extravagant ceremonious farewell believing he deserved it. However, would they then have put him in a crowded graveyard even though, in reality, his perception of the end of his life was different?

Tutu was always very vocal about protecting the environment and creating a difference for the next generation.

As a true visionary, here is what he had to say about global warming during the Copenhagen United Nations Climate Summit *back in 2009.*

> The final measure of a generation's courage is the memory of what they have done. We must live in memory. As the generation that pulled humanity back from the brink of catastrophic climate change, droughts, floods, and water shortages are already on the increase because of climate change. Science has spoken on the urgent need to tackle the challenge. Now, it is time to listen to our consciences. There is a clear moral imperative to tackle the causes of global warming. We're part of nature. Yet we alone can act. Our destiny must be as guardians of the earth, not users and abusers of the only home we have. We all have a responsibility to learn how to live and develop sustainably. In a world of finite resources. We must make peace with this planet.[2]

It makes sense that a person with this mindset would want to depart from this world with the utmost respect for the planet. Hence, he chose Flameless Liquid Cremation, and chose an environmentally friendly and green method of disposition for his human body.

Here is what he had to say about his death.

> I have prepared for my death and have made it clear that I do not wish to be kept alive at all costs. I hope I am treated with compassion and allowed to pass on to the next phase of life's journey in the manner of my choice.[3]

---

[2] "A Call to Climate Action from Desmond Tutu," Living on Earth, accessed September 28, 2022, https://www.loe.org/shows/segments.html?programID=22-P13-00001&segmentID=6.

[3] Desmond Tutu, "When my time comes, I want the option of an assisted death," *Washington Post*, accessed September 29, 2022, https://www.washingtonpost.com/opinions/global-opinions/archbishop-desmond-tutu-when-my-time-comes-i-want-the-option-of-an-assisted-death/2016/10/06/97c804f2-8a81-11e6-b24f-a7f89eb68887_story.html.

This shows how crucial it was for him to be sent off from this world on *his terms*, and by *his choice*. The impact he was leaving on the world truly mattered to him. Indeed, he was a man of great character, caliber, and vision. He deserved all the praise he got in his lifetime. His ideas on how to effectively orchestrate society at large and conduct ourselves personally deserve to be implemented. He made a difference, he achieved practical results, and his accomplishments were many.

He was a good observer and listener, and his success might have also come from his unifying and uplifting belief that, as he said, "We're part of nature. Yet we alone can act."[4]

Desmond Tutu led an inspiring life and left the world the same way by setting an example for others. *He acted.* His decision to choose Flameless Liquid Cremation was widely covered internationally. This shed more light on the subject and raised awareness about this new burial option.

People were interested to know why a person like Desmond Tutu rejected other methods of disposal like ground burial, above-the-ground burial, or traditional cremation. People were surprised to see a religious man choosing a nontraditional approach.

The fact is that he understood why Flameless Liquid Cremation is a better alternative to regular cremation, and above-ground and in-ground burials. He was a pioneer even in this realm.

Desmond Tutu realized that the FLC process uses no fossil fuels. As mentioned before, it has been estimated that this procedure consumes only one-tenth of carbon emissions released by regular cremation.

In-Ground Burial

With in-ground burial, decomposition is extremely slow and takes many years for the process to complete. Additionally, bodies in the ground eventually leak, and if they have been embalmed, this cancer-causing fluid enters the environment. Other issues include worms, the cost of the casket, the grave plot, the cement structure usually placed under it, the expenses for the headstone, perpetual grass cutting, and so on. Estimates are that, in the United States alone, interning people uses over thirty million board feet for hardwood caskets, more than 100,000 tons of steel for caskets, and over 800,000 gallons of cancer-causing embalming fluid.

Similarly, there are plenty of negatives to regular cremation. Caitlin Doughty, a mortician, calls the equipment "behemoth fire machines belching natural gas." The statistics on the amount of materials emitted into the air during cremation are astounding. In the United States alone, it is responsible for 360,000 metric tons of carbon emission through flame-based cremation yearly.[5]

---

4 "A Call to Climate Action from Desmond Tutu."
5 Becky Little, "The environmental toll of cremating the dead," National Geographic, published November 5, 2019, https://www.nationalgeographic.com/science/article/is-cremation-environmentally-friendly-heres-the-science.

In addition, many people are unaware of the complete procedure of regular flame-based cremation. The process needs to be halted in the middle, and the doors of the chamber must be opened to ensure that the flames are reaching every inch of the body and are burning correctly. Workers must poke at the body's remains with a rake to ensure it is being consumed by the flames as completely as possible.

Pacemakers must be removed before a traditional flame-based cremation process can begin. Pacemakers have batteries that may cause an explosion. On the other hand, no such issues exist with Flameless Liquid Cremation. In fact, what is left of any items that might have been implanted in the body are fully safe to handle, are clean, and are probably even reusable.

Do not be afraid of DEATH!

Get out of the carton and LIVE your life, concentrating on the here and now!

Enlightenment is understanding that most things in life are not important.

Enlightenment is living without fear.

Enlightenment is awareness.

Enlightenment is understanding that whatever you give out, you will receive in return.

Enlightenment is understanding that what you have learned so far is not necessarily true.

Dr. Paula Sunray
Sunray Healing Haven and
National Interfaith Seminary

CHAPTER 5

An Individual's Transition Through Time and Space

"You have changed" is a statement everyone probably hears multiple times in their lifetime. In fact, you have probably said it to many people yourself. For instance, when you suddenly see someone you have not seen in years, you might greet him or her by saying, "You look so different! I could hardly even recognize you." You might say this when you meet a child in the family you have not seen for a few months. In this instance, you might look at him or her and exclaim, "Oh my! Look at you! You have grown so much!"

If you think about this for a minute, you will observe that our own bodies go through a lot of changes. Just picture a baby and an adult. We are born so small and fragile, dependent on others for our every need, and then we grow up to become strong and independent adults.

For all people, it is a fact that our bodies constantly change as we grow older.

Do only our physical bodies evolve, grow, and then shrink (in old age), or is there perhaps something more to it?

You might think that you are the "same" person you were ten years ago, or even last year.

In addition to the evolutions of our physical bodies, our mental and emotional states are in constant flux as well. More or less, our memories are relatively fixed. The knowledge we gained through education and life experience stays with us as well (more or less).

People often progress through many different stages in their life and go through hardships, strong emotional connections, failures, joy, sadness, and victories. How can we still be the "same" people after all of this?

One can say that an individual undergoes constant transitions in life in mind, spirit, outlook, personality, and experiences *as well as* in the physical body.

Details about Our Bodies

It is a scientific fact that our bodies do not remain the same as time passes.

Since humans are made up of matter, we have a zillion atoms (a technical term) residing inside of us, and they continue to evolve, alter, and morph into something completely different all the time. By the time of our death, our bodies have 100 percent *completely* changed over and over, again and again, many times.

This would mean your body is continuously changing, even as you sit here reading this book.

This fact about the rejuvenation of the body was discovered in the 1950s when scientists observed subjects after feeding and injecting them with radioactive isotopes. The body's rejuvenation is why our skin flakes off, and nails and hair keep growing even after we cut them. Our DNA's structure is probably the only thing in our body that remains constant from birth. When something goes wrong with that, the human body opens itself up to cancer.

Deepak Chopra, an Indian-American author and an alternative medicine expert, emphasized in one of his talks how our body goes through many changes every day. The changes we all undergo are an ongoing, unfolding process. We go through it daily, as a child grows inch by inch taller involuntarily. We drink water and flush it out of our body via perspiration or urination. Most importantly, think about the fact that millions of cells die in our bodies every day and millions are generated in replacement. Furthermore, the everyday processes of eating food, shedding waste, and using up energy changes uncountable atoms in our body.

It is safe to say that physically, you will be an *entirely* different person when the coming year ends.

If you are sitting here, wondering how you have changed so much over the years (physically, emotionally, and spiritually), remember that it is a natural and expected process. There are many stages we all go through in life until death. It is the circle of life, and we cannot deny it.

Deepak Chopra made the point that even our bones also undergo a continual change process.

Our physical body moves, uses up energy, gets food and some cells grow, and some cells die throughout the day. With every breath we take in, we inhale some atoms from the environment in the form of oxygen, and in the very next second, we exhale some parts of our atoms into the environment, as carbon dioxide. This demonstrates one of the many change cycles of the human body. Perhaps this explains the reason for miraculous healings. There have been numerous cases where people were diagnosed with a fatal disease, like cancer in its final stages. Doctors would state there is nothing that can be done. Later results, however, show that the patient's body had somehow treated itself and rid the entire disease from the system. Perhaps the constant change of atoms in our body contributes to this unexplained, mysterious, and spontaneous healing.

Although medical science today knows a great deal, not knowing how people heal solidifies the fact that our bodies are incredible and have abilities that we may not be able to fathom even in this era.

We also do not know everything about space and time.

Astrophysicists have told us that they are comfortable telling us how our solar system will unfold in time. Although they do not know what gravity is, what dark matter is, or what dark energy is. Although they are debating whether the universe is expanding, expanding at an accelerating rate, or if it will reverse itself and will start collapsing. By observing many stars, they are certain that the sun will fade out in about five billion years during a "slowly expanding cataclysmic process.". More on this later, in the next chapters.

One can look at the human body as a vessel in constant flux; we grow and evolve until suddenly there is no life left in us. We succumb to death just as naturally as we evolve, because death too is a natural process. All these changes are just a part of life, a process that is slowly leading us towards death.

As renowned author Gail Sheehy states in her book *Passages:* "Each of us stumbles upon the major issue of midlife somewhere in the decade between 35 and 45. Though this can also be an ordinary passage with no outer event to mark it, eventually, we all confront the reality of our own death. And somehow, we must learn to live with it."

Truth be told, no one likes thinking about death. It is the *big* unknown.

Many people believe in a religion, and each of these has a take on what happens after death. Some people do not believe in a higher authority. Here we will *not* wade into reincarnation, near-death experiences, life regression hypnosis-driven studies, or going to heaven, purgatory, or the other place. If you are so inclined, we urge you to look into these for they do offer concrete approaches to understanding and coming to grips with this thing called death.

As for the author, it might be worth stressing that Flameless Liquid Cremation brings comfort, peace of mind, and some serenity as far as thinking about all of this.

Young people rarely think about death. They are in the prime of their lives. They have aims and goals to reach, so who has the time to dwell on death? As one grows older and experiences the death of close relatives, it slowly starts to creep into a person's mind. Eventually, one realizes that there is a need to come to grips with the inevitability of it, and that it will be everyone's turn one day.

Witnessing the death of a younger person is especially difficult. Here is someone planning the next five years, fully engrossed in hustling towards success. Suddenly, there is the death of this person who was rushing around, working hard to retire in his or her sixties, and enjoy life afterward. Yet all at once, the person's life stopped, and all those dreams evaporate into thin air. You probably will be confronted by this type of situation and start questioning your life as well, asking *How long am I going to be here?*

Humans are naturally fearful of the unknown. Perhaps that is why death is such a scary part of our lives. As far as we know, no one, as yet, has come from the beyond to tell us what it is like. It is all just speculation at this point.

There comes a time in every person's life when he or she has to come to terms with his or her eventual parting from this world. Despite the fact that it is a big unknown, people eventually will have to come to grips with reality, and somehow internalize and accept the fact that their lives will end one day.

Nevertheless, it is not an easy process; the journey is long and, at times, for some people, quite depressing. If you come to this realization at a young age, it can be an exhausting progression. On the positive side, coming to grips with your mortality can provide a catalyst for success in life. You see, accepting the reality of death can be quite powerful. It opens you up to new perspectives on life itself. Some people start seeing things differently, and live their lives more powerfully. Life is limited, yes, but a miraculous blessing.

Some people do not want to think about it. One can live a full and busy life without confronting mortal fate. It might be difficult to accept the concept of dying, and all that it implies, if you have kept brushing off these thoughts until the very end.

Of course, if you are lucky enough to become a senior citizen, then entering this phase of life brings a new set of plusses and minuses. This chapter of life brings us ever closer to the end of our lives. As we go through every one of our life phases, we are taking a step toward our ultimate end. As each chapter (childhood, adolescence, leaving your parents, getting a job, getting married, and so on) closes, another chapter begins to unfold until we reach our old age, and it is time to close the book and put it down.

As it happens, people are afraid also of just simply getting old as well. Just some of the things that scare people are loneliness, sickness, and financial instability. Seeing your friends leave the world one by one is hard. It makes a person feel more isolated. Life without your friends and loved ones can be hard. In a way, this can become a way for a person to accept the end more easily.

Predictably, losing strength and getting sick is undoubtedly also difficult. Slowly losing your independence and freedom can be stressful and a hard pill to swallow.

Those people who reach old age and are diagnosed with terminal diseases have extra challenges, like thinking about and anticipating pain, hospital bills, long, drawn-out medical procedures, and so on. Sometimes it makes them wonder if they were better off with early death. As unfortunate as that is, they find death more comforting and appealing than the pain they must surely soon endure.

Of course, some people take a more optimistic approach. They believe that every day they lived is a blessing. Death can happen to anyone at any time. Therefore, getting old is a privilege that many don't get to experience. We should live as fully as possible.

Victor Hugo, the famous French novelist, said in his book *Les Misérables*, "It is nothing to die; it is dreadful not to live."[6]

Death is part of our lives. It is a package deal, one that we cannot deny or circumvent. There is no point in fighting it. The only thing that is a constant in this entire universe *is change*.

We are not free to choose when and how we die, *but* we can decide on how we bid the world farewell.

This is why Flameless Liquid Cremation has become a preference for people, once they find out about it. In those locations where it is available, this process is overwhelmingly selected by family members for their deceased loved ones. Once more and more people are aware of it, the author predicts it will eventually become **the dominant** *way that mortal remains will be handled*.

For those people who had selected this process for a loved one, this will probably be their selection as well. They will want to leave the world on their own terms. They will choose a method that is the best *of all the bad options*, and one that makes sense economically and environmentally.

One can talk about transitions on many levels. What happens to a human body (or even a pet's body) as it melts back into nature? Will the process take decades (if buried in the ground) or a few hours (if cremated)?

It might be worthwhile to again mention that, for the author, Flameless Liquid Cremation brings comfort, peace of mind, and some serenity. To be placed into the ocean is not as final as one might believe. The last batch of atoms that made up the body of the author will undergo a wild ride.

What other transitions will unfold after we have died?

Will our earth and the solar system around the sun also come to an end? Let's explore this further in the next chapters. Buckle your seatbelts.

---

[6] Victor Hugo, *Les Misérables*, Wikisource, accessed September 29, 2022, https://en.wikisource.org/wiki/Les_Mis%C3%A9rables/Volume_5/Book_Ninth/Chapter_5.

CHAPTER 6

Physical and Metaphysical Aspects of Death

Some components of our identities will be still left behind. They live on with our children, in the memories of our friends and co-workers, in items we built, and so on.

Of course, we are not buried or cremated the moment we die. Our body does not shut down suddenly all at once. It is a relatively slow process, almost like a computer shutting down.

Our body slips away slowly with each passing breath.

Scientifically speaking, death is declared once brain activity ceases. This results usually from a lack of oxygen, once resuscitation efforts cannot revive circulation and breathing. In hospitals, doctors must follow specific criteria before declaring that a person is dead. Factors they consider before formally making the announcement include absence of pulse (no heart activity), absence of breathing (no lung activity), absence of reflexes, and absence of pupil response to light.

Traditionally, it was believed that a person died the moment the heartbeat and breathing stopped. It is more complicated than that. Some people have been submerged under cold water for over thirty minutes, unable to breathe, and yet have survived. Some Indian mystics can stop their hearts or be buried for a long time, without science being able to explain how they do it.

Doctors often look for other signs before declaring death. Once death has taken place, the body's muscles relax, which is why the mouth falls open. Muscle joints in a body become limp and flexible.

If you have ever witnessed the death of a person, you may have noticed that the body starts looking a little deformed. This happens because the muscles in all areas have relaxed. This also makes the skin sag, and the joints look more prominent. The thumbs in both hands start to curve in toward the palm and small finger. Urine and, at times, feces are passed because of relaxed muscles. A few minutes after the heart stops, the body starts looking pale because blood circulation stops. Liquid slowly starts finding its own level. Since the body is usually lying flat, fluid slowly starts accumulating downward because of gravity. Furthermore, body temperature decreases, leaving the body cold to the touch.

All of this happens within an hour. In the next two hours, the muscles begin to stiffen, starting from the face. The organs, one by one, start shutting down. This is why surgery needs to be immediately planned if the deceased was a registered organ donor.

This is how our physical bodies shut down. Slowly, each part of us stops operating. With lack of oxygen, the cells of our brains also die. However, is that it? Is that lights out?

This book is intended to be neither spiritual nor religious. You must find answers to these realms and questions yourself.

Some people confuse the brain, mind, consciousness, and soul. These do not necessarily have physical restrictions. Our spirit/essence/psyche is not enclosed somewhere. It just exists. Where does it go? Where do these types of energies go? Some say our consciousnesses go into a deep sleep, some say we are resurrected, while some say we wind up in heaven, or the other place.

If you are interested in afterlife concepts, you may want to read the story of the great Houdini. Houdini was a renowned magician and an escape artist who tried to expose the fakery of mediums. He thought mediums were taking advantage of people who had lost their loved ones and were making fools of them with fake attempts at contacting the dead. Houdini promised his wife that he would return from the dead, if at all possible. He would do so in order to help debunk mediums and prove that someone cannot contact or communicate with people who have passed from this world. Houdini and his wife Bess came up with a code. When he died, his wife consulted many psychics, mediums, and spiritualists from all over the world. She even held séances every Halloween to try to contact him. A few years later, a medium named Arthur Ford claimed to have cracked the code. Bess revealed that the code was correct and even released a public statement. However, a friend of Houdini's went to Bess to tell her that the secret code was not so secret. A devastated Bess took back her statement, and several years later gave up trying to contact Houdini. She said, "I now reverently turn out the light. It is finished. Good night, Harry."

This true story might make you think that perhaps the conscious mind dies along with the body. If Houdini could not do it, it cannot be done. Perhaps a soul no longer has the will to do things it would like to do.

An even bolder school of thought says that maybe our minds or souls are moved to another vacant vessel. Perhaps we all just switch and shuffle as we die and are reborn. Maybe we even select our parents.

There have been attempts to, under hypnosis, guide people back in time into previous lives. One can read up on these efforts, if interested. For instance, many people claim they have thoughts and memories that do not belong to them. These visions are of real places and people and, much to the shock of the public, in some cases were allegedly proven true. Some start speaking in a language that has not been around for over 300 years. These are fascinating, and do open up questions about the cycle of life and death. For example, there have been incidents of children as young as five who claim they are not the people others claim they are. They insist that they have lived past lives and are now alive in another body. Are these merely fake claims, or are there things we do not know that we do not know?

CHAPTER 7

Our Eventual Ends

Previously we discussed how our transition toward our ultimate end begins at birth. Obviously, as we get older, we move closer and closer to our death. The journey is a one-way ride.

Here, we will discuss what is going to happen to our bodies in the short term and the long term.

Humans are the only sentient beings that can reflect on our own demise. HAL, the computer in the 1968 film *2001: A Space Odyssey,* had a nervous breakdown after he read the lips of the two astronauts discussing turning him off. HAL understood what it meant to have the plug pulled on him.

We will let you reflect on faith, spiritual understandings, and belief (or disbelief) in religion. The spiritual realm is *not* what we will discuss here. However, it might be beneficial, sooner rather than later, for each person to come to grips with his or her understanding of whether he or she will retain some form of consciousness after death—whether some aspect of the person will go on.

THE HUMAN BODY

ELEMENTAL COMPOSITION

Helmenstine, AnneMarie, Ph.D.
"Chemical Composition of the Human Body." ThoughtCo, Feb. 18 2021,
thoughtco.com/chemical-composition-of-the-human-body-603995.

Flameless Liquid Cremation accelerates the transformation of the human body

- All the soft tissue will be absorbed into the liquid effluent which will wind up in the sea.

- The bones will remain, and be placed in an urn. (To be turned over to the family, or at their request . . . If living near one of the coasts - also cast into the Ocean when the liquid effluent is taken out to sea.)

Atoms That Make up a Human Body

Let's think about all this from a different perspective. We all know that, in addition to water, there are many different components that make up our bodies.

Atoms are often absorbed / dissolved in water. All over the world, this phenomenon is an on-going process. Atoms in water can migrate far and wide. This constant moving and spreading is because of ocean convection currents, and the cycles of evaporation, wind-driven clouds, and resulting rain leading to streams, rivers, and so on.

We inhale and exhale millions of atoms every day. Would you believe that some atoms in our environment may even be from historical personalities like Jesus, Sri Krishna, Augustus Caesar, Muhammad, or even William Shakespeare? As we inhale air, we could be taking in some atoms that were a part of these people.

According to Deepak Chopra, not only is this possible, it is statistically probable. Do we have some past personalities in us through those atoms? Perhaps on some mystical level, this might be a concrete connection with people of the past, and that is how such claims as reincarnation are postulated. We all might have a few atoms within each of us from the actual bodies of great historical figures from the past.

Let us repeat this hypothesis: that there is a high probability that each of us has a few atoms from those who were once alive: Jesus, Sri Krishna, Augustus Caesar, Muhammad, or even William Shakespeare.

The implications of this are huge, especially if you believe in the power of homeopathy. This body of knowledge has shown that even an infinitesimally small amount of matter can have a huge influence on the whole organism.

Not only are there mind/body phenomena at work, there are studies also regarding body/mind influences as well. We will let philosophers, statisticians, and people with religious faith work out the details.

No matter what, you must admit our vast universe works in profound and wondrous ways.

DNA 101

Our DNA has many similarities with other creatures of the world. When we talk about the connection and energy that flows in the universe, it is all somewhat interconnected, including plants and animals. Researchers are finding organic matter on asteroids. Some scientists theorize that originally early DNA was introduced to earth from some outside source on a meteorite. This kick-started life on Earth.

Did you know that we share 60 percent of our genes with bananas, 70 percent with fruit flies, 80 percent with mice, and shockingly over 98 percent with chimpanzees? How incredible is that?

Cosmology 101

Today, our technology is so advanced that we know what will happen to our planet and the solar system billions of years from now. These are not just speculations. Astronomers have spent years working on theories, experimenting, and observing our universe. They have uncovered a lot of knowledge as to the fate of the Earth.

Scientists now believe that everything on Earth, the moon, Venus, and Mercury will be eventually absorbed into the sun. As the sun continues to heat up, it will eventually fully consume all of the Earth and the other planets into itself.

Similar to human beings, the solar system will eventually die as well.

According to scientists, in about five billion years, there will come a time when the sun will run out of the fuel (hydrogen) that keeps its gases burning. Eventually, it will enter its red giant phase. As the sun enters this stage, it will slowly expand, and with this final cataclysmic process, it will take in the planets closest to it. The entire world, as we know it, will melt into the sun. As the sun expands, it will enter Mercury's then Venus's orbit. The expansion of the sun will be so strong and powerful that Earth will eventually be pulled into it as well. That means the atoms that once made up you and me will wind up there.

When considering the Earth's end, think about how similar it is to cremation. The Earth will give up its atoms. It also will be reduced to its basic elements. As Carl Sagan famously said, "we're made of star stuff."[7] He could have also meant that not only do we come from that source, but we will wind up there eventually as well.

The end of the solar system resonates with the process of Flameless Liquid Cremation. It emphasizes a universal connection, a typical birth-life-death cycle.

In addition to this, think about how after dying, no matter which burial method one chooses, we will all blend into the sun one day. The disposition of our bodies may differ, but eventually we all become one with nature. In the long run, all our atoms will come together and merge back into the cosmos.

Ultimately, our burnt-out sun itself will participate in the clashing of galaxies, as our Milky Way collides with the next closest large galaxy, Andromeda.

It will not be wrong to say that everything has a final end. For humans, other creatures, planets, and even our Sun, cosmic plasma will be the fate of all.

The atoms of people buried at sea become part of what scientists call the universal solvent, in other words, Ocean Water. When it is time for the end of the earth to unfold, the water in

---

7 *Cosmos: A Personal Voyage*, episode 1, "The Shores of the Cosmic Ocean," directed by Adrian Malone, written by Carl Sagan, Ann Druyan, and Steven Soter, aired September 28, 1980, on PBS, https://archive.org/details/cosmos1theshoresofthecosmicocean360p.

the ocean will heat up and evaporate. We will all become "star stuff." In the end, all will be connected. We will all be one.

Recap/Summary/Epilogue

The fact is that Flameless Liquid Cremation is a greener, more palatable approach than any other method. It is a more tolerable way to leave life behind. Let's face it: no option is great.

As this book reaches its end, the author wants to emphasize how natural the Flameless Liquid Cremation process seems, once you realize that all matter and atoms contained on the planet will also have a similar end. Furthermore, you get to make this enormous decision, on how to *expedite* your melting/melding back into the world of the sea. To wind up in a good place.

Where available, the use of Flameless Liquid Cremation is spreading fast. Practitioners feel that it is *the future* of human disposition. In the future, most people will not be buried, but will dissolve in slowly circulating alkalinized water.

At locations available, people are overwhelmingly choosing this approach to after life disposition because it offers:

- Environmental benefits

- Economic benefits (ie: it is as cost effective as "regular" flame-based cremation)

- Speed (and is safe and hygienic)

- Not to mention, offers profound peace of mind

We attempted to provide clear, fact-based information. Now that the awareness of Flameless Liquid Cremation is in your hands, you too can plan. Think about asking for a fast, efficient, economical, farewell; and one that is responsible, as far as the planet is concerned.

We have discussed how atoms and plasma will in the very distant future connect all of us with each other, and how things will play out at our ultimate, mutual, eventual ends.

Flameless Liquid Cremation seems blissful. Is it not a soothing and comforting way to say goodbye to life, *especially when compared to other even less palatable options*?

It is a way to own your fate, to keep the reins in your hands even at the last moment. When we finally let go of life, we will be able to join nature in the most respectful way possible.

The woodcut below, from the sixteenth century, depicts this realm and these mystical reflections in an artistic manner.

A 17ᵗʰ century take on how to figure out what happens after death.

APPENDIX A

Insights on Getting Old

A compendium of accumulated insights on getting old. Some observations and excerpts are from the following discussion threads on www.quora.com:

- How does it feel to be an old man?

- Does the death of friends help people not to fear death as much?

- Do people still want to go beyond 100?

In general, this Appendix presents some sentiments the author feels are worth thinking about!

One way to look at your life is that YOU have *already* "won" a big prize! In the beginning, when competing with millions of upon millions of sperm, YOU "won"!!

YOU beat incredible odds! YOU were the one born! Life is the ultimate gift. Nothing else comes close.

Note: Consider that the average man (like your father), during his lifetime produces over 500 billion sperm!

Sample conversations Sperm might have had:

Sperm Philosopher…   Shakespeare said it best, "To be or…"

Doomed Sperm #1: "Are we there yet"?
Sperm #2: "No! We all have a long way to go, we only just passed her tonsils."

Have something that interests you, to look forward to, someone to help.

Seek out and listen to stand-up humor as many times and as often as you can.

On volunteering, donating money, giving generous tips: "No act of kindness, no matter how small, is ever wasted" (Aesop)

Gratitude is important: "It is not happy people who are thankful; It is that thankful people who are happy"(Author Unknown).

GO for it: "To Get the Most Out of Life, Look Upon It as an Adventure" (William Feather).

On getting and taking care of a dog:

"Dogs Are Not Our Whole Life, But They Make Our Lives Whole" (Roger Caras).

"Dogs Are Our Link to Paradise. They Don't Know Evil…Or Jealousy…Or Discontent" (Milan Kundera).

Generally speaking, you remain "yourself" your whole life. You feel like "yourself" whether you are old or young. Typically, you are the same basic person at 90 as you were at 19. (Our) bodies hurt a lot more, balance is worse, have more trouble seeing and hearing and remembering things, etc. BUT…we are very much "ourselves" inside. Hopefully wiser and more experienced.

People who are "young at heart" appreciate nature whenever they are around it, and love to be outside as much as possible. If one elects FLC (Flameless Liquid

Cremation) and since all people going through this will eventually get "buried at sea"…this will surely happen.

Children always strive to experience new things, to throw themselves into learning new skills and trying new activities. Many adults tend to fear the unknown. We will all, through death…get the chance to have a "new experience."

As death becomes much more of a "frequent" thing, it becomes not as "scary" anymore. If you make it to 80 or 90, your parents have died, maybe some siblings have died, and you've attended the funerals of many friends. You have somewhat gotten "used" to the idea that you may be the next one to die. The word "die" doesn't seem as "frightening" anymore.

As time goes on, it sinks in more and more, that death is inevitable. It is one of the "Passages" author Gail Sheehy in her book "Passages" talks about.

You are not invisible. One can try to look on the outside…as you feel inside. Self-image is important. How you dress makes a big difference on what you project. Older people mostly abandon trying to look younger, but dressing well is something that we can all embrace.

Margaret Manning "Sixty and Me" YouTube gray haired influencer

The Art of Staying Young at Heart Through Fashion - YouTube

https://www.youtube.com/watch?v=MWiNb_SjdSc&t=192s

It is natural to have a motivation to keep on living, no matter what your age. If a person loves life, they might be ready to die tomorrow, but not quite ready to go today.

With age comes wisdom, and one realizes that: Nothing lasts forever. Nothing is meant to. In the whole universe…the only thing that is constant…is change. A scientist would say, entropy increases.

A person's ATTITUDE is very important. There are no "old" men. There are men in old bodies. Some people are already "old" at 30. Some will never be "old".

Attitude is more important than facts. It is more important than the past, than education, money, circumstances, than failures and success, than what other people think, say, or do. It is more important than appearance, ability, or skill. It will make or break a business, a home, a friendship, an organization. The remarkable thing is I have a choice every day of what my attitude will be. I cannot change my past. I cannot change the actions of others. *I cannot change the inevitable*. The only thing I can change is attitude. Life is ten percent what happens to me and ninety percent how I react to it. (Charles R. Swindoll)

When I wake up EACH morning, I am grateful for this next day. I always remind myself of what wise people have taught us…that tomorrow is not guaranteed for any of us.

I appreciate getting old, it is a privilege many don't get to experience. My father taught me to be an optimist. That something good is coming. Enjoy every day, there is always something to be grateful for when a new door opens.

Many aspects of getting older are inconvenient. BUT IT BEATS THE ALTERNATIVE. It does get increasingly difficult to lift heavy objects, put your clothes on, to play the sport you used to…to be as vigorous and active as you were. BUT (stop complaining) for IT BEATS THE ALTERNATIVE.

One thing that Marines learn is that there are no excuses. Make things happen! Old age is just an inconvenience. Figure out ways to still take the actions you need to; to accomplish your goals…in spite of aches and pains…and all.

As time goes on, you will start realizing that many of the things you thought were important turned out not to be too special; AND many of the things you dismissed lightly and even rebuffed sometimes, like love and closeness become more valuable.

He who dies with the most stuff does not really "win." In fact, most of your treasured possessions will end up being donated to strangers.

If you are open to the "spiritual" side of things, read about Near Death Experiences, Life Regression Hypnosis, reincarnation of endless consciousness, etc.

As humans, it is our nature to fear unknown things. This is to be expected. But rolling with the flow…while keeping your eyes open, and having keen "situational awareness" is the best thing we can do. While being administered an inoculation before being put to sleep for a major operation (that I woke out of 5 hours later)… what went through my mind is…Que Sera Sera. When I did "wake up"…I wiggled my toes, to confirm I was not paralyzed. EVERYTHING WAS OK AFTER THAT!

Get politically active. At a recent protest, a young woman held up this insightful sign:

"I am no longer accepting the things I can not change. I
am changing the things I cannot accept!"
(Image was marked as copyrighted by Robert Stuart Lowden 2017)

Some people have found it useful to look at "life" through these analogies:

➤ The party is over, most of the guests have already left, so I might as well go also. Anyway, they are now playing music I do not like, using jargon and gizmos that I fully do not grasp☺

➤ I've had an incredible life. I have seen and experienced unbelievable things. It really would be Ok if I checked out soon. I am at peace and ready to go.

➤ I'm OK, it's all OK, I can let go. It's not that I want to go, just that I am somewhat OK with it.

➤ I think of death as the end of what has been a great adventure. Most people realize that every living thing eventually dies. By the time we reach "really old" status, most of us have come to terms with the inevitability of death. We know it is going to happen to us sometime in the next few minutes, to possibly as much as ten years from now.

➤ _Some_ people have the following mind-set: They have no fear of death, it is the cessation of being. They may not even know when it happens. And once they are dead, they believe that they won't know or feel anything anymore. Lights out.

➤ I have lived a full and interesting life. More or less, I guess I've seen it all. The movie is over, the credits are rolling. I can go now. The feeling of having done lots and lots of "stuff" during my life is incredibly peaceful, satisfying even.

➤ People into "mindfulness" tell us, to concentrate on the "now." You can't control every aspect of your being. Enjoy your time that is given…"the now." Live in this moment. Do not be "worried" about something that hasn't come yet. Live fully today, so that you do not regret yesterday (because of wasted time having overly worried about tomorrow).

Status of Flameless Liquid Cremation by State

For pet and animal husbandry (i.e., farm) use, it is approved and available in all fifty states. For the disposition of human remains, the current status (as of the date of publication) is as follows.

Source Document: StateLegalityProgress2022.pdf from Bio-Response Solutions Inc.

Alabama	Available	Massachusetts		South Dakota	
Alaska		Michigan		Tennessee	Available
Arizona	Available	Minnesota	Available	Texas	
Arkansas		Mississippi		Utah	Available
California	Available	Missouri	Available	Vermont	Available
Colorado	Available	Montana		Virginia	
Connecticut	Available	Nebraska		Washington	Available
Delaware		Nevada	Available	West Virginia	
Florida	Available	New Hampshire		Wisconsin	
Georgia	Available	New Jersey		Wyoming	Available
Hawaii	Available	New Mexico			
Idaho	Available	New York			
Illinois	Available	North Carolina	Available		
Indiana		North Dakota			
Iowa		Ohio			
Kansas	Available	Oklahoma	Available		
Kentucky		Oregon	Available		
Louisiana		Pennsylvania			
Maine	Available	Rhode Island			
Maryland	Available	South Carolina			

APPENDIX C

Bibliography, Resources, References

"A Call to Climate Action from Desmond Tutu." Living on Earth. Accessed September 28, 2022. https://www.loe.org/shows/segments.html?programID=22-P13-00001&segmentID=6.

Cosmos: A Personal Voyage. 1980. Season 1, episode 1, "The Shores of the Cosmic Ocean." Aired September 28, 1980 on PBS. https://archive.org/details/cosmos1theshoresofthecosmicocean360p.

Dignity Memorial. "How Long Does a Cremation Take?" Dignity Memorial. Accessed September 28, 2022. https://www.dignitymemorial.com/plan-funeral-cremation/cremation/timeline.

Hugo, Victor. *Les Misérables.* Wikisource. Accessed September 29, 2022. https://en.wikisource.org/wiki/Les_Mis%C3%A9rables/Volume_5/Book_Ninth/Chapter_5.

Little, Becky. "The environmental toll of cremating the dead." National Geographic. Published November 5, 2019. https://www.nationalgeographic.com/science/article/is-cremation-environmentally-friendly-heres-the-science.

Tutu, Desmond. "When my time comes, I want the option of an assisted death." *Washington Post.* Accessed September 29, 2022. https://www.washingtonpost.com/opinions/global-opinions/archbishop-desmond-tutu-when-my-time-comes-i-want-the-option-of-an-assisted-death/2016/10/06/97c804f2-8a81-11e6-b24f-a7f89eb68887_story.html.

Resources and Background. Recommend looking at the following.

- "Aquamation for Funeral Homes at NFDA 2019" (video on YouTube)
  https://www.youtube.com/watch?v=PUjBGuHvXDU
  In this video, Samantha "Sam" Sieber, Vice President of Research at Bio-Response Solutions, demonstrates the use of the equipment.

- "The Future of Death: Inside the Machine That Dissolves Corpses" (video on Bing)
  https://www.bing.com/videos/search?q=Resomator+%22+alkaline+hydrolysis
  &&view=detail&mid=7B761204310DCB9F73BA7B761204310DCB9F73BA&&
  FORM=VRDGAR&ru=%2Fvideos%2Fsearch%3Fq%3DResomator%2B%2522%2
  Balkaline%2Bhydrolysis%2522%26FORM%3DHDRSC3
  In this video, Dean Fisher, director of the Donated Body Program at the David Geffen School of Medicine at UCLA, describes the process and the equipment used.

- "Our Aquamation from start to finish at Natures Pet Loss" (video on YouTube)
  https://www.youtube.com/watch?v=AL5uHdMPmR8
  This is a Florida facility that uses the technique for pets. The woman talking is impressive for her warmth and the true caring way she expresses herself. Her staff behaves respectfully as well.

- "In the future, your body won't be buried…you'll dissolve" (video on Wired UK)
  https://www.wired.co.uk/article/alkaline-hydrolysis-biocremation-resom
  ation-water-cremation-dissolving-bodies
  This is a detailed magazine article about the process.

"The environmental toll of cremating the dead"

https://www.**nationalgeographic.**com/science/article/is-cremation-environmentally-friendly-her-es-the-science

https://www.**quora.**com/How-does-it-feel-to-be-an-old-man-Do-they-thin
k-about-death-Does-the-death-of-friends-old-men-help-people-not-to-be-
scared-of-death-Do-people-still-want-to-go-beyond-100

Books

- Jastrow, Robert *Until the Sun Dies*
- Sheehy, Gail *Passages*
- *Sister Age* by M.F.K. Fisher
- If you are relatively young (or young at heart), read Aubrey de Grey's *Ending Aging: The Rejuvenation Breakthroughs That Could Reverse Human Aging in Our Lifetime*

APPENDIX D

Final Parting Images to Savor, Embrace, and Comprehend

Here I come

Note: If you are seeing this on an electronic device, please CLICK on the image, then CLICK on the arrow at the bottom.

This simulates how people who undergo Flameless Liquid Cremation will spend "eternity".

NEW BEGINNINGS, A FLIGHT IN THE SUN
Poem by Linda Dietz

That first bright step into the sunshine of
life
begins with the opening of the family
cocoon.
The caterpillar becomes a butterfly
spreading her wings into the world.
What she is today is but a tiny mirror.
of the transformation that is yet to come.
For with time, love, humor and warmth
She is an ever changing masterpiece.
Whether as wife, mother, career woman or
all,
she will find her center of peace.
A place that is hers and hers alone,
the essence of what she is and will be.
Using the instincts that each of us have
to find the good in each other.
to be a caring friend, lover, helper and
playmate,
to listen and share, to laugh and to cry.

With loving support of family and friends,
she takes flight down an unknown road
towards her future,
like the rising of the sun in the east.
Each day filled with new beginnings.
Finding excitement and challenge at each
new turn.
Her flight through life filled with many
happy adventures
and memories to put in her book of life,
as the sun moves along that steady path
across the sky.
When the sun at last begins to set in the
west
and her flight nears its end, she can look
back along her path
and know that she has been everything she
can be
and has done her very best.

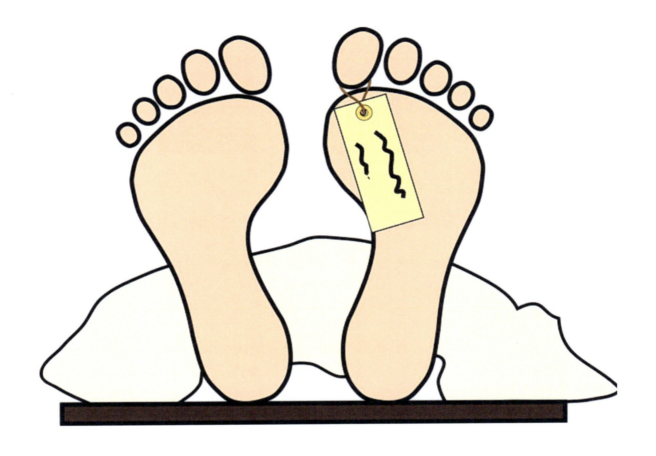

The only thing to do on my "To Do List" is to melt back into the universe, in as efficient, economical, and sustainable manner as possible.

A selection of butterfly quotations

Researched by Jacqui Knight for the International Butterfly
Breeders Association

I only ask to be free. The butterflies are free.
~Charles Dickens

If nothing ever changed, there'd be no butterflies.
~Author Unknown

Butterflies are self propelled flying flowers.
~R.H. Heinlein

**The butterfly counts not months but moments, and
has time enough.**
~Rabindranath Tagore

**What the caterpillar calls the end of the world, the
master calls a butterfly.**
~Richard Bach

**We are like butterflies who flutter for a day and think
it is forever.**
~Carl Sagan

Eventually . . . the atoms of **all** people going through Flameless Liquid Cremation will wind up in an ocean.

For locations near one of the coasts . . . we recommend to have practitioners institute, for **each and every** Flameless Liquid Cremation . . . the following "**Best Practice**":

> As part of the normal, customary, included, bundled, "regular" Flameless Liquid Cremation process, **all** of the liquid effluent will be respectfully disposed into the nearby ocean.

Since this liquid is **100% sterile and non-toxic** . . . if the family requests it, they can be provided with a one gallon sample portion; to be sprinkled in their back yard on tree and/or brush roots. It is very rich in fertilizer type nutrients.

We feel it is **comforting for people to envision** being poured directly into the ocean (ie: a straightforward "burial at sea"). In other parts of the country, who are not near a coast, the atoms of loved ones will also **eventually** wind up in an ocean . . . once the flow of water from the drain, though the local processing plant reaches a nearby river, which will **ultimately** take the atoms of their loved ones to an ocean.

"Old Man" Dancing – Mexican Folkdance

Because of the piece-of-mind and comfort that Flameless Liquid Cremation offers, "old" people can dance not only in Mexico!

An artist's mystical vision of a "gateway" to the Ocean...

and the Eternal Residence of the atoms that made up what we were!

Maxim to live by:
Seek out meme extensions,
extending beyond the confines of
words into images

Created and generously shared by:
Baroco Ferison, Bortsworth, UK
https://pixabay.com/users/barocof-11418167/

I will be there (in the relatively **COLD** water) remembering:

- The **warmth** of the sun
- The **warmth** of my wife

  (FULL DISCLOSURE: *she is not the one pictured here*)
- The **warmth** of my friends
- The **warmth** of such organizations as:

  UNICEF

  World Central Kitchen

  CARE

This is now my new home

... once my LIQUID EFFLUENT (and for me . . . my URN contents) reach the ocean

(i.e.: what remains of me after death)

Note:

This is not just an anti-smoking message, making the point that you are literally "burning up" your life.

But it is also a more general message, that time is marching on, and we have a fixed amount of time left before we reach the final end.

"Eat, drink and be merry"

   – **An old English** idiom, associated with the philosopher Epicurus, and Ecclesiastes 8:15

"Gather ye rosebuds while ye may"   -   Robert Herrick

My Eventual Forever Home

For full disclosure . . . If we have anything to do about it, this is where departed (deceased, dead) people from NJ and NY will be able to spend eternity. (Until everything on earth and the moon "melts" everything into the sun in about 4 billion years from now)

His Owner Has Died and now has Melted Back into the Sea

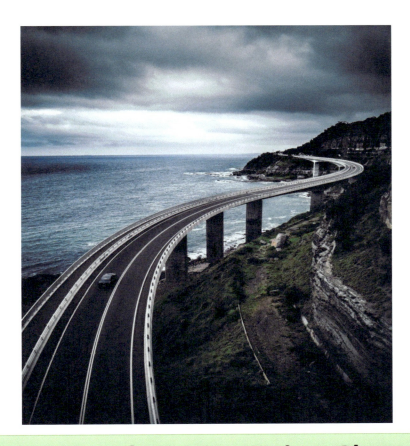

Day or night, when you Drive Close to me (having been cast into the vast Ocean water) - think of me and wave

Printed in the United States
by Baker & Taylor Publisher Services